MAXIMUM GPA IN MINIMUM TIME

MAXIMUM GPA IN MINIMUM TIME

79 Quick Tips for Better Grades
Starting Today

JOSH SILVA

Copyright © 2014 by Josh Silva

MAXIMUM GPA IN MINIMUM TIME:
79 Quick Tips for Better Grades Starting Today

All rights reserved. No part of this publication may be reproduced, distributed, or transmitted in any form or by any means, including photocopying, recording, or other electronic or mechanical methods, without the prior written permission of the publisher, except in the case of brief quotations embodied in critical reviews and certain other noncommercial use permitted by copyright law.

First Printing 2014

ISBN-13: 978-1503080560

ISBN-10: 1503080560

INTRODUCTION

Do you feel like your grades don't reflect your intelligence level? Are you not getting better grades even with increased effort? Do you think if you could become more organized you'd do better in school? Are you doing pretty well but just want to become a little more competitive for admission requirements at the next level? If you answered "yes" to any of these questions, then this book is for you.

I wrote this book to be a very quick read that can provide immediate benefits. While the subject matter might not seem overly exciting, the possibilities of what these tips can lead to is *very* exciting. Who doesn't want better grades, more free time, and a better shot at a good job after college?

Take an hour or two to read over these ideas, and you just might find that tiny time investment pays very large dividends for you. You have very little to lose, and much to gain, so without further delay, here are the best tips I've found on how to achieve your maximum GPA in minimum time starting today…

One

A Little Preparation Leads To a Lot More Free Time

1
Record Your Whole Schedule

At the beginning of each quarter or semester, take the time to record assignments, due dates, and test dates on an easily accessible calendar or planner. A full-year calendar that can be hung on your wall is a good choice. Another option is to cut out the months for the quarter or semester from a monthly calendar so you can see everything at once.

The above strategy can be really helpful, because you can see what is coming up and plan your time accordingly. There is a surprisingly large difference in perspective between looking at a monthly calendar and being able to see the entire quarter or semester all at once. Also, if there's nothing to do or no one around, you might be inspired to look ahead and knock out some work in order to spend your time in more enjoyable ways.

Many students will choose to use a calendar solution on a smartphone, tablet or laptop, options that can also work well, especially for students who are rarely home. As with all tips in this book, you need to find what works best for you, but if you're finding that you're getting behind on work because you're not aware of what's coming up, it could be worth considering the yearly calendar idea.

2

Study If You're Bored to Feel Bored and Productive

Try to use your down periods to get ahead. Admittedly, these are the times when you won't want to work, but I'm not talking about vacations, or necessarily even weekends. I'm talking about times during the day when no one else is around and you're watching TV or sitting around on campus. Keep your books on hand in order to do get work done during these periods. You could do math problems you already know how to do, or gather research materials for an upcoming paper. If you're ahead of the game because you got work done during boring times, you'll be able to relax and enjoy the fun times.

3

Do the Work to Lose the Anxiety

Worrying doesn't relieve anxiety. Action does. Break things into small pieces and chip away at them. If the big picture is too overwhelming, just look at a project bit by bit. If it's still too overwhelming, break it down even further.

Starting a project is usually the hardest part for most people. A good remedy for such procrastination is to set up your homework or project as soon as possible. For some reason, getting going on a project seems to be much easier if 1% is completed as opposed to if nothing has been started. Even if it's a twenty-page paper, start by writing the title, your name and date. You can stop there, or very likely, you'll realize that since the step only took a minute, you also have time to write out a rough outline and maybe some initial ideas. You might realize that you could do a bit more at that point, and before you know it, you've made substantial progress.

 Momentum is created from a series of small steps, so let this force work in your favor by setting things in motion early.

4

Plan Free Time to Have More of It

Plan your "free" time as much as you plan your studying. We can only focus on one thing for so long, and it's good to take study breaks. If you're faced with a project that seems overwhelming, consider not only taking study breaks, but planning them ahead of time.

 The above strategy really depends on your work style, though. If you're a "marathoner," taking a break might kill your valuable momentum; if you're a "sprinter," taking a short, fun break could be all you need to regain your energy and power through the rest of the work.

 Also, working for a finite amount of time seems less stressful than working for an open-ended amount of time. Be wary of watching TV or playing video games during any breaks, though, or you might sap your energy. Go for a walk outside, shoot some hoops, or have a light snack. Most importantly, set a time to get back to work so you can regain your focus quickly.

5
Rein in Electronic Communication Time

You might want to consider checking your email only once or twice per day and setting time limits for social media and texting. Tim Ferriss has a great discussion on time-wasters in his #1 best-selling book, *The 4-Hour Workweek*. He suggests checking email twice per day at pre-set times.

Email, social media and texting are such a part of the life now that they are hard to avoid, but they can also waste *a lot* of time. If you have a large amount of work to do, it might be helpful at times to stay offline and to turn your phone off. Another good strategy is to take care of any electronic communication when you only have a short amount of time between classes.

6

Choose to Not Connect on Last-Minute Scrambling

Making connections with others on healthy shared interests (such as sports or hobbies) is an important part of life. People also connect on negative things, though, and one of these is procrastination. Many students wear procrastination like a badge of honor, bragging about how late they waited to do a paper and how they were up late all night doing it. People enjoy hearing this, because many of them waited until the last second, too, and it makes them feel better if others are in the same boat. Is it better to fit in this way, or to get a project done a couple of days early and be able to do what you want?

Rise above the false sense of connection and feel the relief of finishing a project early. Better yet, encourage friends to get their work done early so they'll have more free time as well.

Two

Maximizing Study Time: When, Where and How

7
Choose Where You Study Based on Your Goals

Where you study can be very important. Introverts might find this to be true more than extraverts, as introverts tend to be more easily distracted by things such as noise, but even extraverts can benefit from fewer distractions. If you want to study with people to get to know them better, go for it, but you may need to schedule additional time to study on your own if studying with others distracts you from learning.

Go against the grain to find effective times and places to study. Go to the library early on a weekend night, or early on Saturday or Sunday morning when most people are still asleep. Empty classrooms can also be great places to study. Be creative in terms of where you study, because the more creative your idea, the less likely others are using it, resulting in less distractions for you.

8
Develop Flash Memory

Flash cards can be a great learning tool, but there are a couple of tricks to keep in mind in order to use them effectively. Students will often create a large stack of cards to memorize and go through the stack over and over in order to learn the words and concepts. There's a better way.

After you guess the answer on each card, mark down on the back how well you knew the answer. An easy way to do this is to mark either "Y" for Yes (you got the answer easily), "M" for Maybe (unsure until you looked at the answer), or "N" for No (no idea). The second time around, mark the cards again. If you mark a card "Y" for a second time, remove the card from the deck, as the answer has sunk in. Repeat these steps until you get a "Y" two times in a row for each card (or three times if you're more cautious).

A more efficient version of the above strategy is to be honest with yourself about the answers you absolutely know, and throwing the cards with these answers to the side right away. By using the second strategy, you can narrow the cards to the ones you're having trouble guessing correctly more quickly.

If certain cards take you several tries to get right, keep them in a separate pile in order to review them again quickly right before the test.

Many students go through whole decks of flash cards over and over, but you'll probably find the method described above will save you time and enhance your retention of difficult test topics.

9

Think of Whether Study Groups Work for You

Separate study time from social time. Study groups can be useful, but many offer only a little learning along with a lot of social interaction. Be honest with yourself about whether you learn things better in a group. If you do learn better in a group, then figure out at what point during the studying cycle this is true. For example, do you gain a better grasp on concepts initially in a group, or does a group setting help firm up what you've learned (by providing the opportunity to ask about what you don't understand and helping others with what you do understand)? Also, when evaluating the usefulness of a study group, be sure to take into account the amount of time spent in relation to what is accomplished.

∞

10

Sense the Sense That Makes Sense for You

Figure out your learning style and then make the best use of it. How do you "get" things best? By listening to the professor and not having the distraction of taking notes? By taking extensive notes? By copying the notes you took in class a second time? By reading? By teaching others?

If you're not sure which sense works best for you in terms of learning, try a few of the above methods in an easy class. Be careful not to test different learning strategies by doing something like not taking notes in a tough class and then realizing how stuck you are when it's time for the first test. Pay attention to what works for you instead of just doing what everyone else seems to be doing.

If you're really not sure what your learning style is, enter the words "learning style," or something similar, online and you'll find plenty of links explaining different learning styles along with self-tests that will help you discover what works best for you.

11
Use Words for Number Problem Problems

If you get to a tough problem, especially in a subject such as math or physics where there's one correct answer, try writing out in words what you don't know (i.e., what is making you stuck). Then, write out what you would need to know or do to be able to get past it.

You can make tough problems seem less overwhelming using this method, because you are breaking the problem down into what you can do and what is causing you to get stuck. For example, you might write, "there are three variables, only one is known, and I don't know how to find one of the missing variables." Then, you can write that potential solutions are as follows: 1) call Dave from class; 2) go to professor's office hours; 3) scour the book; 4) try an online search for a similar problem. If you can't find a solution right away, move on to the problems you *can* do and get back to the tough ones later. You can also see if you keep running up against the same obstacles or if a subsequent problem helps you understand what you were missing before.

12

Focus to Get More Done Quicker

One of the most important skills that must be self-taught is the skill of sustained concentration. Being able to get work done despite distractions is a good skill to develop, and concentration is an extremely important skill to have for difficult problems.

These ideas might seem self-evident, but how often do people really concentrate on one thing for more than about ten minutes without distractions? Focused concentration is how big problems are solved, whether within a group or by an individual. Not only are the solutions that come out of concentrated work often better, but concentration also functions as a time-saver. Try to find a quiet corner of the top floor of the library or another spot where you know you can consistently focus when needed, and you may find that work that used to take you a couple of hours can be completed in a half-hour.

13

Don't Study As Much As Others… or More Than Others

Set your own standards for studying. Be careful not to fall into a trap of basing how much you should study on how much other people are studying. This is a trap for a few reasons. First of all, some people are incredibly smart and don't need to study much. Second, some people don't care much about their grades and don't study much. Third, you don't see any one person all the time, and some people study at odd times. Lastly, some people might still be caught up in the idea that studying isn't cool and sneak off to do it. Base your efforts on what's required for each class and your personal goals. Let your grades, not the efforts of others, be the measure of whether you're doing enough.

14

Reduce Clutter to Reduce Stress

Does clutter really *cause* stress, or just add to it? That's debatable, but there definitely seems to be a relationship between clutter and stress. If you don't believe it, think about getting some work done while you're in a cluttered room, and then think about the same work again an hour later after you've cleaned the room. Does it feel a bit different? Maybe even *a lot* different? Physical space can affect how we feel mentally. Clearing up clutter provides a sense of space and can take the edge off of overwhelming feelings that can come up when you're faced with a big project. The more obvious benefits are being able to find your papers and having enough room to work!

15

Learn By Teaching

Learn by teaching others. Make sure you grasp the material first (or at least be honest about what you don't know). Teaching can be a *great* way to get material to sink in better, and also to figure out if there are areas in which you still need some brushing up. You can also do a trade by teaching a subject you know really well to a student who can in turn help you with another subject.

16

Learn Using Headphones

Reading isn't always feasible or safe in certain

situations, but the time you spend in these situations doesn't need to be wasted. Try recording the most important notes for a test and listening to them in your car or on the bus. If you record your notes for a test in order to listen to them, you're not only making use of extra time that would otherwise be wasted, but you're also learning from multiple angles. First, you *hear* the professor in class and *write* down the notes. Next, you have to *read* the notes out loud in order to record them. Finally, you *hear* them again on the recording.

It will take some time to record the notes, but by using time you otherwise wouldn't be able to use for studying, and by making yourself learn through writing, reading, and listening (twice!), you'll have a much better chance of absorbing the material. Of course, if you don't have as much time, a much more direct method would be to just tape a lecture and listen to it in the places described above, although this method wouldn't include as many forms of learning.

Three

Go Ahead, Test Me

17
Use Study Guides with Confidence... Usually

Trust, but verify, the accuracy of study guides. In most classes, study guides really do distill the subject matter into all that needs to be studied for a particular test, though some professors stray from what they include in a study guide. Speak with past students about how your professor operates, or look for online reviews of professors, especially if reviews are available for your particular class.

I received a painful lesson about study guides in my very first quarter of college. I trusted that a study guide in a particular class would accurately reflect what would be on the test, but unfortunately that wasn't the case at all. Even worse, I was not aware that the professor in this particular class had been using the exact same test for several years. Consequently, some of the members of fraternities and sororities in the class had copies of the test. These students drove up the curve because they all got such high scores. (On a tangential note, members of fraternities and sororities can be very good sources of information about classes and professors because they are able to pass down information in a continuous stream each year.)

I found my bad experience in that one class to be the exception, though. In most classes, the study guides were very accurate outlines of what would be on a test. Just be sure to check with the professor, reviews, current students, or past students to verify.

18
Memorize With Mnemonics

Make use of mnemonic devices in preparing for tests. Mnemonics are easily memorable, catchy sentences where each first letter matches the first letter of what you need to memorize. The trick here is to make sure there's something about the word you use that will really help you remember the word. The simplest way to do this is to have the first two letters of the word match as opposed to just the first letter. For example, use the word "always" to represent Alabama. If you only match the first letter, it can quite a bit more difficult to remember which word the substitute is supposed to represent.

If you don't want to go to the trouble of making up your own mnemonic devices, you can do a web search to easily uncover many possibilities for common concepts. For example, Wikipedia currently has a whole page dedicated to chemistry mnemonics.

19
Crack the Code

Try to figure out the political and philosophical biases of professors. These biases often come through in lectures and in the wording of questions on tests (and in answers on multiple choice tests). The books a professor assigns might also provide clues. Don't search for biases too hard if they're not on the surface, but sometimes it's fairly easy to pick up some extra points on a test when biases are recognized. Just knowing that college professors tend toward political correctness can add a few points on every test in some classes, especially in political science and history.

20
Retain Tests for Future Gains

If possible, keep your midterms in order to review them for finals. Each professor has a distinct style, and skimming back over a test can help you remember what types of questions were asked. You can also see if you can spot any particular patterns, especially in multiple choice tests. Was "all of the above" the correct answer in seven out of the eight questions in which it appeared? If so, it's probably a good bet on questions for which you're unsure of the answer. Does the longest answer tend to be correct? Multiple choice tests often provide many ways to "crack the code" if you can dedicate some time to investigating patterns in the answer choices.

Some professors create better tests than others, and you can gain a big advantage by looking for patterns in early tests in order to do better as the term goes on. If you're not allowed to keep a midterm, at the least you can usually see the test on the day it's returned and make note of as much as possible about the questions and answers while the professor is going over the test in class.

21
Effectively Tackle Scantron® Tests

If you are allowed to write on a test's question sheet, cross off answers you know for sure are incorrect. In order to take the test quicker, you can mark your answers on the actual test the first time through, and then transfer them to the answer form afterward. If you know an answer, circle it on the question sheet and move on. If you don't know the answer on a particular question, cross off the answers you know are wrong and move on. Don't spend too much time on any one question the first time through the test.

On the second time through, transfer your answers to the Scantron® form as you go along, starting with the ones you already circled, and making your best guesses on the others. (If you know you have plenty of time, an even better method is to go through a second time to mark all of your answers on the test sheet, and then to go back a third time to transfer each answer to the answer sheet.) Be sure to keep an eye on the clock in order to have time to transfer answers. Another benefit to this method is that it will help you avoid the common problem of having answers on the Scantron® form not match up with the questions on the test sheet because of skipped answers.

22

Don't Cheat, Even If Cheaters Sometimes Win

Don't cheat. Just don't do it. The only person to whom it should matter whether or not you "get away" with cheating is yourself, meaning that in reality you never get away with it. Keep your integrity in check and use the tools from this book to do well on tests no matter what other students do to raise the curve by cheating. If you need a more practical reason, don't do it because a C on a test is better than the consequences of getting caught, which would be a 0 on a test at best, or very likely, expulsion.

23
Avoid Temptation During Crucial Times

You will benefit from keeping your environment predictable before a test. Try going off to a quiet part of the library or joining up with a study group to go over the test. If you're especially prone to being distracted by video games, partying, or anything else that will make your thinking hazy, plan ahead to avoid such temptations. Planning what you'll do for a few hours leading up to a test will help provide peace of mind. The last thing you'll want is to feel anxious about what might come up that could affect how you do. Schedule a time and place to be during the time leading up to a test, no matter what else might happen, and you'll put yourself in the right frame of mind to do your best.

24
Avoid the Convenient Excuse Trap

Don't skip studying the night before a test in order to have an excuse for yourself and others for why you got a bad grade. If you keep your ears open, you'll see just how common these excuses are. It may sound corny, but it actually takes courage to try your best. If you study hard and fail, it could be a blow to your ego. If you go to a party instead, you can just convince yourself and others how much better you would have done had you studied.

You might also be tempted to see what you can pull off with raw intelligence, and you may do very well. Just know that the top people in any field almost always work hard on top of having talent. Our culture seems to be fascinated with natural talent, but it doesn't get people far unless they practice. Put in the time and effort to succeed and you might surprise yourself with how much you can achieve.

25
Prepare for Admissions Exams

Whether you will be taking the SAT to get into an undergraduate program or a test like the GMAT to get into a graduate program, make use of every resource you can to prepare for the test. Any bookstore will have several choices of books that can be used as study resources, and these books are well worth the time, especially when they include practice tests. Do every practice test you can, while keeping the environment and time restrictions as close as possible to what you'll experience when you take the actual test. Don't stop taking the practice tests until you can score even higher than your goal and you can get the test done in less time than required, because it's very likely you won't be quite as relaxed during the actual test no matter how much preparation you do.

Other resources to consider, if you can afford them, are classes and private tutors. If you are able to use these resources, especially private tutors, you might be able to speed up your learning process and achieve an even higher score. Also, if you have an auditory learning style, taking a class might be more effective for you than using a book. No matter which method you use to prepare for admissions test, make sure you do prepare extensively, as specific strategies do exist for each test that you can use to achieve a bump up in your score.

Four

Accept Your Laziness to Get More Done

26

Accept Your Laziness to Be Less Lazy

Discipline is a valuable trait, and getting your work done no matter how you feel is one of the most important study habits. Therefore, fighting laziness with all your might would seem a worthwhile effort. However, such effort can cause increased resistance. Instead, accept that your desires have a lazy aspect to them. Why does this mentality work? Because it's human nature to want to get as much done as possible with as little work! If you wait to work hard until you *want* to work hard, you're not likely to get much done. In fact, the urge to work hard might not ever come. Accept that you're lazy and do the work anyway. There's no need to waste time and energy trying to convince yourself that you're not lazy. Viewing yourself as a hard worker isn't a prerequisite to getting a lot of work done.

During the times when you don't have the energy to work hard to get a lot done, and you're not up against a crucial deadline, accept your lack of energy and get a little done instead of fighting it and not getting anything done at all. At least this is a good strategy in some cases, leading us to the next point about different types of studying.

27
Study Differently for Different Circumstances

Learn to differentiate between types of studying in order to make efficient use of your time. For example, you might be able to make flash cards while watching TV, but you would probably need a quiet atmosphere to memorize the flash cards. You might be able to knock out simple math problems if you're already familiar with them, but you'll probably need to focus in order to learn new concepts. Think about what the goal of a study session is, and you should be able to figure out the ideal type of environment in which to complete the work.

28
Pay Attention to Your Energy Patterns

Note the times of day or circumstances in which you do and don't have energy. This observation will help with both classes and studying. Try to avoid taking difficult, boring classes in the afternoon if you usually feel sleepy at that time (as many do). If you consider your energy patterns when you register for classes, you might find that you have an easier time in class and studying outside of class.

29
Study When You Will Instead of When You Should

When are you *really* willing to study? Doing something mellow the night before a big study day is a good idea, but fooling yourself into thinking you'll study during a time when you've never been productive rarely works. If you can study on weekend nights, that's great, as these will be the quietest times by far in places like the library, but don't miss out on a social life completely if you're not really going to get much done anyway. While this book focuses mostly on grades, "who you know" tends to matter quite a bit when applying for jobs and internships, so be sure to develop as many good connections as you can while you're in school.

30
Set Deadlines to Feel Less Stress

Try setting a deadline a few days before your due date, and don't stress until that time. You won't waste as much time stressing yourself out about procrastinating if you know the date by which you need to start. Write down what needs to be done, and lists tasks in order to work backwards, setting small deadlines along the way. Don't ruin your weekends by worrying about work you weren't going to do until Monday night anyway. Enjoy your free time instead, knowing that the work will get done soon.

By using the strategy described above, you'll gain the psychological benefit of knowing you don't *have* to get the work done until a certain point. The trick is that it can be much easier to get work done if we feel like we don't *have* to get it done, and of course if you feel like doing extra work ahead of time, it will only benefit you. Nothing is as relaxing as finishing an assignment early and then not having to worry about it at all.

31
Act First to Feel Motivated

Motivation comes from action, and not the other way around. If you wait to act until you're motivated, you might never stop waiting! As best-selling author Robert Ringer said in his book, *Action: Nothing Happens Until Something Moves*, "Contrary to popular belief, you don't need to be motivated to act. If necessary, *force* yourself to take action, and motivation will follow."

The thought of *starting* work will hardly ever sound appealing, but getting into the flow of work can actually be enjoyable, and finishing work always feels good. We tend to exaggerate how bad work will be in our minds, but then once we start on something it's often not as bad as we feared, and that's when the motivation and energy start to pick up. Sometimes motivation won't come at all, and you just have to grit your teeth and work through an assignment. If motivation is to come, you often won't know until you've already started working, so just get started and see if that extra boost will help you get your work done.

32

Develop Discipline Instead of Worrying About Motivation

Concern yourself with being disciplined instead of being motivated. Motivation comes and goes and is hard to control. The most productive people are disciplined. They do what they need to do whether they feel like it or not, and in fact, they realize that it's often what they feel like doing the least that will provide the greatest benefits over the long term. Natural motivation is great, but not necessary, and realistically it might not ever come.

Be careful not to read too much into lack of motivation. For example, you might not be motivated to do your biology homework, but this lack of motivation doesn't necessarily mean you don't want to be a doctor. (On the other hand, if you volunteer in a hospital and hate it, this feeling is probably something to pay attention to.)

In life, discipline may be the most important skill to develop. People stay in shape because of their discipline regarding eating habits and exercise, they become skilled in a musical instrument from disciplined practice, and they advance in their careers from the discipline it takes to get the job done. The earlier you can develop this crucial skill, the more effective you'll be, and the easier it will be to have discipline spill over to other areas of your life. Discipline is largely a matter of practice, so work at it the same way you'd work at developing any other learned skill.

33
Use Small Amounts of Time to Achieve Big Results

Look for uncommon times to do homework. You might be surprised to learn how much more studying you can pack in if you get a little creative. Some potential places to get extra study time in are at a baseball game, on the bus, in long lines, at the laundromat, in the cafeteria, outside on the grass, at the beach, and in a class before it starts. Some times to consider are early before everyone else is awake, early Friday night while you're waiting to go out, any time you're waiting to meet up with someone, and at half-time at other sporting events.

Bring work with you whenever there is any chance of having some time to fill so you don't miss out. For example, you could carry a paperback from an English class with you if you're going to the post office or doctor's office where the wait could be an hour or more. Think about what kind of work you might be able to do in certain situations, and plan ahead to make the most of potential opportunities.

34
Use Parkinson's Law to Your Advantage

Parkinson's Law states that "work expands so as to fill the time available for its completion." This law can be used *very* effectively. When study time is open-ended, and nothing is scheduled afterward, it can be very stressful, as it really feels like there is no end in sight. Consequently, students often procrastinate in such situations, because the task seems too daunting. However, there is an alternative, and you may find it very effective, even though it seems very simple on the surface.

One application of Parkinson's Law to studying could be to find pockets of time *right before* something fun is scheduled. If you have an hour (or even 20 minutes) before a party, or a game, or really anything you're looking forward to, use that time to get in some quick studying. The pain will be over before you know it, and you'll be so focused to get to the fun event that you may find you're much more productive than usual during this time.

Although a little different from Parkinson's Law, another way you can use the tension of an anticipated event to your advantage is to set a specific amount of work to get done and to not go to the event you're looking forward to until that work is done. Then you'll really focus!

35
Record How You Spend Your Time

Consider recording what you do every hour of each day for a week. This is an extreme step, and I can pretty much guarantee it's the one that very few readers will actually do. But if you're willing to take the time to do it for only one week, it could help you not only in school, but for the rest of your life. Why? Because you'll see how much free time you truly do have. And trust me, unless you're working 40 hours and taking 20 units, you probably have much more free time than you think.

If you sleep eight hours a night, that translates to sleeping 56 hours out of a total of 168 hours during the week. That leaves 112 waking hours during the week. Take away 20 hours of classes per week from total waking hours, and the balance is 92 hours. Take away two hours per day for eating and hygiene for a total of 14 hours per week, and that leaves 78 hours. That's a lot of time! It's good, and even necessary, to use some of these hours for rest and relaxation. If you find yourself killing time as opposed to spending it productively, though, you'll see how much more you can get done by figuring out what your time wasters are and limiting them in favor of more productive activities.

Five

Group Work

36
Draft Your Team Wisely

Be very selective when choosing a team for group projects (if given the choice). Not only will being selective in choosing a team help you get better grades, but it can also help preserve your relationships. A great friend might not put out much effort in group situations, straining your relationship with that person. If you're unsure about how to handle not wanting to work with a friend, just tell that person you know too many friends who had their relationships affected by being in groups together, and that being friends is more important than being on the same team. Your friend might still be put off and think you're making a big deal out of nothing, but this still might be better than risking a whole semester of tension.

37
Scout Potential Group Members

If you ask around, you might be able to find out who works well in groups and who does not. This information can be very valuable! In programs that require a lot of group work, learning the reputations of others is fairly easy. The key is to find out about the extremes, meaning who's the best in groups and who's the worst. By working hard and doing a very good job on group projects early on yourself, you can develop a solid reputation as well as good relationships with other strong students who will want to work with you again. If you're able to find a strong core group of potential team members, you could even plan to take classes together where you know you'll be able to choose your own team.

38
Grind It Out

Work in groups is rarely distributed evenly. A student used to getting C's knows that by joining a group with A-students, he or she can do C work and still get at least a B. The A-students will be disappointed, but the C-student will get a B for doing C work. Sometimes professors allow students to grade others within their group anonymously. Even then, some students just don't care, and even being graded individually by their teammates won't motivate them to work hard. At times it's just a matter of putting your head down and getting through project or class. Keep in mind the end goal of getting the best grade possible and don't get too caught up about what is fair.

39

Consider Working as Just One Man or Just One Woman

For the reasons in the last section, you might choose to avoid group work when possible if you want more control over your grades. Classes with group work often end up taking more of your time as well. Exceptions exist, but between coordinating a project, ineffectively trying to get work done during meetings, and then trying to piece the project together, group projects can take an inordinate amount of your time. Also, because groups usually meet more than necessary, and it's difficult to find times when everyone is free, you'll have less control over your free time, as any time you have free is expected to be available for meetings.

40

Test Early and Be Thankful Later

Consider giving each member of your team a short assignment as early as possible to gauge each person's work ethic and quality of work while there is still time to adjust team roles. If you can figure out the relative strengths and weaknesses of each person early on, you'll be able to develop a good strategy to mitigate weaknesses. It's much easier to deal with potential weaknesses at the beginning of the quarter or semester than to be surprised by them right before a project is due. On a more positive note, you might find some very strong skills in a quiet or humble group member that can be put to much better use than if assignments were handed out randomly or if people were asked to volunteer their own strengths.

41
Establish Guidelines Right Away to Save Time Later

At the very beginning of a group project, establish style and format guidelines for each member to follow. Putting contributions together from different people might sound like a simple task that can be taken care of at the end, but often it's not simple at all and can be time-consuming. Distribute an email or paper containing the font type and font size of text, headlines, and sub-headlines; margins on all sides; and what type of exhibits should be used. (Better yet, distribute a template with all of the preferred settings incorporated.) Keep your team's formatting consistent at the beginning and you will be less stressed and rushed at the deadline.

42
Project Management Gets Results

Consider using a project manager for a team project, especially if you're on a large team. If you have enough team members, you can also assign the job of editor/collator. In a small group, the project manager can do the editing and collating as well. If a project manager is not used, you run the risk of all the individual pieces not flowing in the end. Setting guidelines is a very good idea, but it's not enough on its own.

One caution is that team members can become jealous of the project manager early on, because the project manager won't have nearly as much work to do in the beginning of the term. However, this person often ends up spending more hours than any other team member on the project, and most of these hours come at the very end of the term, often at the expense of sleep. If you really want control of a project, project manager is a great position for you, but just be ready for the stress and late nights it will likely entail. The more a team can break each group member's assignments down into shorter pieces with frequent deadlines, the better off the project manager will be, because any surprises at the end will at least be manageable.

43
Get Goals Out Into the Open

At your first team meeting, have each group member talk about the grade he or she would like to target for the project. People are usually fairly honest about this subject. If you are able to choose your own team, and you see major discrepancies among members, you might still be able to switch teams. If not, you can at least find out what you can expect out of each team member.

If you know that you're not a particularly strong student compared to the others in the group, the other students in your group will really appreciate it if you're upfront about your strengths and weaknesses. Most students realize that each student has a different set of skills to offer. The important point is that everyone has *something* they can contribute, and most group members will judge each other more on effort than output anyway.

Six

The A-Student's Secret and Not-So-Secret Resources

44
Take Advantage of Office Hours

Professors' office hours can be a very useful resource, but you wouldn't know it by how few students tend to show up for them. If you just show up to office hours, not only will most professors want to help you, but they'll often give you tips on what will be on the next test. Also, professors can explain things in a way better suited to individual learning in office hours than in class.

Listen to what your professors say to do to succeed in the class, and if they don't say, just ask. Most professors appreciate when students show interest and really want to learn, and showing up to office hours is an easy and effective way to communicate interest. Not only will going to office hours likely lead to understanding your class materials better, but showing effort can really make a difference in terms of getting the benefit of the doubt on a test or paper.

45
Cheat on Your Professor

Your professors are not your only resources for learning a subject. Some professors chose their occupation in order to teach, some to do research, and others for the job security. If you need help in a subject, search out the professors who enjoy teaching, even if they don't teach your class section! Professors from other class sections won't be able to tell you what will be on a test, but they might be able to help you with the underlying concepts.

As long as they're not overly busy with their own students, professors who are passionate about a subject will almost always be willing to help. Find a genuinely flattering reason to ask for help, such as hearing of a professor's good reputation from other students. If asked about your professor, stay neutral and say you thought learning from a different angle might enhance your understanding.

46
Learn Everything You Can From Your English Teachers

One of the most important skills you can pick up that will set you apart from others is the ability to write well. Spending as little as one hour with a good English professor who can *really* go over your writing with you and give you tips about grammar and style can be very valuable. Going over each paper you've submitted with a professor for a whole quarter or semester will make an even bigger difference. Don't assume any needed corrections on your papers will be made. Many professors don't bother to correct more than the most obvious errors.

Writing well is one of the most effective ways

to stand out from your peers in classes, in job and graduate school applications, and later on, in the working world. The books *Elements of Style*, by William Strunk and E.B White, and *Woe is I*, by Patricia T. O'Conner, are great references to keep on hand. The latter is an easy, quick read, and if you can believe it, actually fairly entertaining. Plenty of online resources exist as well, and they can be found easily by searching the word "grammar."

47
Question What He Said She Said He Said

Go one step further than word-of-mouth information. Why? It's often not accurate. If you've ever played the game "telephone," where a story is passed from one person to another several times and is barely recognizable at the end, you'll understand why. Talk to students about classes, but take the extra step to look for professor reviews, online syllabi, etc.

It often only takes one extra small step to move ahead of others. I've said similar things many times in this book, and repeating this idea is no accident. Not much pays off more than doing even a little bit more than what most people are doing, or to think just a little more creatively than others. If you're willing to think more independently and to try things others aren't doing, you're likely to be happily surprised with the results.

48
Ask the Aces

Seek out students who did well in the classes you're going to take. These students will have a much better grasp of what it takes to succeed in these classes than the students who didn't do well, and they will likely know the pitfalls to avoid better than the students who didn't do well. Why? The students who did poorly never "cracked the code" of the class. Find the students who did well in order to have the code cracked for you before class even starts.

Seven

Tips That Couldn't Be Forced into Other Categories

49
Rise Above Food Fog

Don't underestimate the effect of your diet. Does sugar make you wired for an hour or two, but then you crash afterward? Does starch make you sleepy? If you're doing your undergraduate work during the typical ages of 18-22 or so, you're probably able to get away with a lot in terms of eating poorly and not sleeping much, but maybe not as much as you think. Cafeterias usually offer fairly poor choices in terms of what to eat, but do your best. If you're able to eat mostly real foods and lay off the junk, you might find that you're able to focus better and that you feel a bit sharper when taking tests.

50
Avoid Depending on Drugs to Not Have to Depend on Them

Food can affect people tremendously, but it's even more important to be very careful with stronger substances. Don't do anything before a test that is different than what you would do otherwise. If you normally drink one cup of coffee per day, having an extra one is fine (although staying off stimulants of any sort is probably even better).

Stay current with your studies and you won't need to abuse your body with stimulants to make it through late night after late night. Be especially careful about taking anything that comes in a pill or powder to increase your energy, because in the long run you could be setting yourself up for a world of trouble by using hard drugs. Choose rest and a healthy diet in order to have a clear mind and enough energy to get your work done, and you'll set yourself up very well for life after college when your body won't be quite as forgiving.

51
Go to the Front of the Class

If you feel uncomfortable sitting front and center in class, just sit in the front but off to the side. This tip goes along with the idea of separating your school work from your social life. You can talk to friends in a class before or after class, but during class try to sit in a spot where you will have minimal distractions, usually meaning up front. If you're sitting next to someone who constantly wants to talk to you, and you feel rude telling that person to stop, make up an excuse to sit somewhere else if needed, or just reply less and less until that person gets the hint.

Students who are less focused and who talk more still tend to sit in the back even in college, so the closer to the front you can sit, the less distracted you will be by them. Leave the distractions outside of class hours, and you'll absorb the material much better. As a bonus, when a professor sees your level of focus, he or she will be even more willing to help if there is something you're not quite grasping.

52

Control Time

Use two alarm clocks. I can't think of a simpler, yet more important, tip than this one. Your professors (and future employers) aren't likely to believe that your alarm clock "didn't go off." They'll know you pressed snooze too many times, or set your clock incorrectly, or just slept through the alarm. The main point, though, is that there is such an easy and cheap solution to make sure this doesn't happen that it should be common for everyone to use two alarm clocks. One of the two clocks can be plugged in, but be sure that at least one of the two is battery-operated so a power outage during the night doesn't reset the clocks.

53

Choose Not to Snooze

If you can, get in the habit of waking up when the alarm first rings. In other words, don't use the snooze alarm. Getting up immediately is kind of like pulling a bandage off, where quick, intense pain can be better than long, drawn-out pain. Pressing snooze usually makes people feel drowsier, but the most important part is that pressing snooze once can too easily lead to pressing it twice... then three times... then eight times. Also, once snooze has been pressed, it's a small step to turning the alarm off completely.

I realize I'm probably over-exaggerating a little here by essentially describing the snooze button as the "gateway" button, but if you can train yourself to just get up right away when the first alarm goes off, it will become a habit that becomes easier and easier over time. Getting up when your alarm first rings will also help ensure that you'll get up in time for work, where the consequences of showing up late will likely matter more than being late for class.

54
Manage When Life Gets in the Way of School

Illness, family problems and other issues come up from time to time and may cause you to miss a test or assignment. Getting ahead on projects can help prevent problems to a degree, but there might be times when you're blindsided and it's nearly impossible to get things done or to make it to class for a test. In these cases, the first step you should take is to contact your professors as soon as you know that you won't be able to do your work. In cases where the missed assignment or test could really affect your grade, you'll probably have to approach your professors to find out what options you have, if any, to make up what you missed.

There are two fairly easy things you can do that will increase your chances of being granted a favorable option—take responsibility for missing the work and offer a solution. If you take responsibility for missing the work, your professors will see you as a responsible adult. You're the one who is asking for special treatment, and if there is any way you can think of to make it easier on the professor for you to make up the work, make sure that you express this. If you can learn this lesson well, you'll be a big step ahead of most of your peers when it comes to the working world, where bosses look much more favorably upon employees who provide potential solutions when presenting problems.

55

Choose Enthusiasm and Optimism Over Envy and Cynicism

Make a point of avoiding envious or cynical people, and instead, try to hang out with positive, enthusiastic people. Find supportive friends, family, and mentors, and minimize contact with negative people. Be especially careful about sharing big plans with negative people who might try to discourage you.

One important caveat is that you'll need to learn to differentiate between negative people and people who want the best for you, yet have valuable information to share. If you know someone who is generally very positive and supportive, it's actually very important to pay attention to the rare times when that person does bring up an obstacle to consider. Here's an example of how this could look:

Student: I'm going to be changing my major to art next semester.

Pessimist: Art? Who are you, Picasso now? All that tuition is going to go to art? There's no money in art, everyone knows that.

Supporter: Art sounds like a fun major, and you've always had an aptitude for it. Have you thought about what classes could go along with art to make sure you'll be able to support yourself, such as taking marketing or computer science classes?

56

Seek the Uncomfortable Truth

Try to go to where the answers are, instead of where the answers are most conveniently found. Many students miss out on finding good career information because they stick to talking to those with whom they are most comfortable. Who are the best resources? People working in a particular profession are a good bet, but possibly even better are those going into a particular career whose parents are doing the same thing. The son or daughter of a doctor will likely not only know about what the profession is like, but also have a good sense of the internships to seek out, the classes to take, and research opportunities.

It only takes a little extra research in life to get much better answers, but you do have to take the extra step. Many people search online or ask those closest to them, but the most complete answers are a step or two beyond these methods. Don't wait to be pushed to do this, because it won't happen. In fact, "pushing" happens less and less as time goes on. Elementary school teachers are usually encouraging, while only some high school teachers are, fewer college professors are, and even less people in the working world are. Learning will be increasingly self-directed as your schooling and life goes on, and you can really get a jump on the competition at a young age by being willing to seek out the best information, no matter where it's found.

EIGHT
College: The Big Transition

57
Interview Your Roommate

If you plan on living in a dorm freshman year, call or email your assigned roommate before school starts. If it's obvious the person isn't a good fit for you as a roommate, try to switch your living arrangements as soon as possible, as it's usually much easier to make this change early on in the school year.

If you're worried about offending the person, realize that he or she is likely to find you just as incompatible. You don't have to live with someone just like you, but you will want a roommate with habits you can tolerate. For example, if you like quiet and going to sleep early, and your roommate prefers playing music in your dorm room until 3:00 am, it's probably not going to be good for you or your grades.

58
Do Some Registration Reconnaissance

A little research before registering for classes can make all the difference in the world. Registration usually takes place during the middle of each quarter or semester, and it can often sneak up on you when you're really busy. The best time to do research on classes and professors is at the *beginning* of each quarter or semester when your work load is fairly light and you can easily find out which of your acquaintances are taking particular classes. If you write down their initial thoughts on classes and professors, all you would need to do later on is double-check this information right before registration. Even if you don't go beyond finding out their initial thoughts, you'll still have much more knowledge than most students. After all, the really bad professors often make themselves known right away!

Consider using Microsoft Excel or an online program to track information on classes and professors. Being able to sort information easily and in many different ways can be a very powerful tool. You might even want to consider working on this spreadsheet with several other students who have similar goals in order to increase its effectiveness. You can serve as the central information-keeper while they gather the information for you, or better yet, set up a web-based program or forum that anyone you give access to can edit.

59
Create Weekend Options

Early on, try to make friends who don't party too much so that you will have various social options on the weekends. This strategy will become very important when you have a lot of work to complete on weekend days. If you can't find people to hang out with in the dorms, consider clubs or intramurals, especially those that focus on studying or activities that involve waking up early on the weekends. Clubs that have to do with outdoor activities are a good example of the latter.

Making friends with people who aren't into partying every weekend doesn't mean you have to avoid parties. What it means is that on nights when you have a lot to do the next day, your choice won't be limited to staying in by yourself or staying out much later than you wanted and possibly not feeling so great the next morning.

If you make non-partying friends early on, you signal to others that you enjoy hanging out with different kinds of people. By keeping your social options open from the beginning, you can avoid the awkward feeling that you have abandoned some people in favor of others.

60

Pick Your Roommates When You Can

Be very careful when choosing roommates once you have a choice, typically meaning after your freshman year. Many good friendships have been lost because two or more people didn't function well as roommates, and this added stress and tension can easily affect grades. Think not only about you'll want to live with, but also who would be the best roommate. These can be very different measures! If you spend all of your study time outside of your dorm/apartment/house, your roommates might matter less, but they still affect your overall stress levels (and sleep time). You can always find parties or go hang out at the "fun" houses, but knowing you have a predictably quiet place to sleep can really help minimize stress and increase your energy during the day.

61
Skip Class Sparingly

College is the first time most students are away from home for a decent length of time. I can guarantee that you will see a wide range of how well this is handled! You'll see students who were shy in high school decide to break out of their shells and be outgoing. You'll see students who got in trouble a lot in high school suddenly mature and not go out until they finish their homework. These are the positive changes. You're also guaranteed to see many students who can't handle having so much freedom all at once, and these students often slip quickly. Although it's often things like alcohol or other drugs that are the source of the problems, what usually gets them in trouble in terms of school is skipping classes.

Try to always go to class unless there's a really good reason *not* to go (versus only going if there's a good reason *to* go). Consistently attending classes is especially crucial the first year or two, because you can really get in trouble by skipping classes early on and making it a habit. Generally, only the toughest classes can still be failed if a student attends every class, but *any* class can be failed if enough classes are missed. After a while, you might figure out which classes you can skip here and there, and you might even make better use of the class time you skipped. In general, though, the simplest way to stay on track is to just go to every class unless you're sick or there's a true emergency.

62

Create Calm, Even When Surrounded by Chaos

Try earplugs. It's amazing just how much sound the good ones block out. You might have to try a few different kinds of earplugs to find the ones that work best for you. They'll probably never feel completely comfortable, but the benefits will likely outweigh any discomfort. Introverts might appreciate earplugs even more than extraverts, as introverts tend to get distracted more easily, but even extraverts need quiet study time sometimes. Earplugs can also be very beneficial when it comes to sleeping, especially in the dorms. Strategies such as using earplugs to gain more control over your environment can be very useful, as they rely on your own actions instead of on you trying to change the actions of others.

63
Outline Your Path and Work Backwards

List the classes you will (or might) want to take to fulfill your degree requirements along with the general education classes that interest you the most. The earlier you can create this list, the better off you'll be, as you can gather notes on these classes and their corresponding professors along the way. Also, by knowing which classes you want to take early on, it will be easier for you to plan ahead for classes that are only offered once per year as opposed to every quarter or semester.

Your list of desired classes should be easily available to you so you can enter notes whenever you learn new information. The secret here is that the amount of extra work to gather this information is actually very small, but the payoff can be very big! (You'll notice that the previous sentence just might be the theme of this book.)

NINE
Major Ideas

64
Don't Get Weeded Out

Most majors tend to have one or two "weeding out" classes that occur early on, even if schools won't necessarily admit such classes exist. The purpose of these classes is to see whether students are really cut out for a particular major. A common mistake is for students to assume classes in a major will get increasingly tough. The reality is that weeding out classes are often the most difficult in a major, so if you really want to stay in a particular major, don't get too discouraged by a tough class early on.

The important part is to find out which classes within a particular major are known as the weeding out classes. Word on these classes often gets out quickly, so students who started along with you might already know which ones they are. If not, the best source is likely to be older students in your particular major. These students could possibly be professors' assistants in some of your classes. The next possibility would be to check with an advisor within your major.

Once you know which class serves the purpose of weeding out the weaker or less serious students, you can put it in perspective. You'll know that you'll probably have to work quite a bit harder to get a good grade in that class, but you'll also know that poor performance doesn't necessarily mean you'll do poorly in that particular major or that you should change majors. If you don't identify the weeding out classes, you might mistakenly assume that all the classes will be that difficult.

65
Try Potential Majors Early

Switching majors at least once, if not several times, seems to be a college tradition. The key is to start this process as early on as possible. One good way to test out majors is to take classes that fulfill both a general education requirement and a requirement for the major you want to evaluate. This strategy ensures you're not wasting any classes, as all of the classes count toward your general requirements.

Since general education classes are lower-level, another way to test out potential majors is to sit in on a few upper-level courses in each major that interests you. Most professors will be happy to let you sit in on a class or two, and if the class is big enough, you might be able to just walk in and take a seat without asking. By checking out the upper-level courses, you'll get a much better sense of what's expected of students and the difficulty level of the major.

Do some research early on to avoid spending an extra year or more in college because you switched your major late in the game. Changing your mind about your major ten times while you're still doing your general education work is a lot less costly in terms of time and money than changing it just once after you've completed most of the work in a major you no longer want.

66
Keep an Eye on the Future

Why are you in college? Are you planning on going to graduate school? If so, is it the grades in your major or your overall grades that matter? How you will be evaluated is important to find out, as it can really affect where you should direct your efforts. For example, let's say that you want to go into a field where graduate schools mostly look at your major GPA. In this case, it might be worth it to put in extra time on a tough major class even if it means you slip a little in a couple of general education courses. On the other hand, if it turns out that it's your overall GPA that matters most, you won't want to waste all of your time on one major class in order to get bumped up a half-grade if it means dropping down a half-grade or more in two or three other classes!

If it's a difference between passing or failing a difficult class, that's a different story, but just be aware of how much time you're spending on each class and what you expect to be possible in terms of grades. Overall GPA and a chosen major tend to be the most important factors for many graduate programs, but not always, so do a bit of research to see what graduate schools are looking for so you can plan your time accordingly.

67

Ask Yourself What Comes Up Over and Over for You

Pay attention to your long-term feelings and goals. If you've always wanted to be a doctor, don't let one class deter you. You may experience times when a tough class or quarter will make you want to switch to an easier major, but do your best to stick with whatever will move you toward your career goals. You can get a job in a recreation department with a biology degree, but you're not likely to get a job in science with a leisure studies degree!

The rewards of a particular major tend to come late in your schooling, not early, so it's important to stick with the major you really want. Besides the weeding out classes, other early classes might not only be tough, but they'll also likely be general and possibly even boring. The upper-level classes tend to be the rewarding and interesting ones. Plus, the true reward comes at graduation time, when you can proudly look back on sticking with a tough major that sets you up for a good career or graduate school.

68
Major for Work, Minor for Fun or for Insurance

Try to use your major to prepare for a career, as this is the main point of going to college. If you think classes in a particular major are interesting, but you're not sure what type of work they would lead to, consider using a minor or electives to take these classes. A minor can often be enough to qualify for work in a particular field, but even if it isn't, you can always take more classes later as a second major during your undergrad years or even after you graduate. Being able to name particular classes you took in a certain major on your resume can provide a boost to your credentials.

There are thousands upon thousands of former students who regret getting a "useless" degree in a basic major they chose because it was easy, or interesting, or someone told them that all that mattered was getting a degree, regardless of major. Don't believe this lie! Yes, getting a degree is valuable in comparison to not getting a degree, and many companies won't hire for certain positions unless the applicant has a bachelor's degree.

When you are starting out in your career and have very little experience, your degree serves as a substitute for experience. After a few years of real-world experience, the major won't matter as much anymore, but at first it can definitely make a difference.

69
Build Your GPA with Forgettable Classes

Getting into graduate school typically consists mainly of two things: 1) grades and 2) standardized test scores. Even though I stated earlier that some graduate schools care more about overall GPA and some about major GPA, be careful of just focusing on your grades in your major, because you might end up wanting to go to graduate school for something different than you originally expected.

A very effective way to build up your overall GPA is to seek out the easiest general education classes. Students tend to talk about these classes quite a bit, so they're usually not too difficult to find. If you're unsure of your major, you'll need to weigh taking easy general education classes with taking general education classes to test out various majors. If you're dead-set on one major, though, and know exactly what you want to do with it, maintain your focus by taking the easiest general education classes so you can put your time and energy into the classes that really matter to you while building a solid foundation for your overall GPA.

70
Pave the Road to Your Future with Internships

Depending on your major, one of the most important steps toward finding a job once you graduate is to get good internships during one or more summers. Ask older students in your major how internships work in your field, or better yet, ask an advisor. Internships are often overlooked by many students, but they look great on resumes. Also, the earlier internships can be done, the better, as they will give you a sense of what work in a field is really like. You'll get a sense of the career track, the amount of hours people work, the dress code, and maybe even salary information. Internships are a great way to get the experience companies want, giving you an advantage once you graduate.

Ten

Things You Will Realize After
College That You Can Learn
Now Instead

71

Charge Ahead to Open Doors

It often works better to plan for something specific and change your mind than to "keep your options open." When you are moving toward *something*, it's easier to figure out what you do and don't like. It might seem paradoxical, but doors only tend to open when we're moving toward a goal, even if it turns out the opportunities are for something tangential or even completely unrelated.

When you try to figure out everything in your head, there can be answers that you are missing. Also, when you think that something isn't possible, you'll tend to find answers that reinforce this negative belief. When you think instead about what you want, and decide to figure out *how* these goals would be possible to achieve, that's when doors can open for you. Decide what you want, and then draw upon the resources and knowledge of others. You may find your choices are much more expansive than you previously thought.

72

Follow Dreams or Money or Both. Just Try to Get at Least One!

Some books and people advise students to "follow their dreams," while others suggest to go into whatever career makes the most money in order to have the resources to enjoy life outside of work. Both arguments have their merits, but the important thing is not to go into work you don't like for low pay! Often students really have only a vague sense of what various jobs pay, but it's worth it to take the time to research this early on in college.

If you can go into a field you like, one big benefit is that you'll be more likely to stick with it and put in the time and effort to really do well. Being able to take care of yourself financially is very important, but work takes up so much of the day that you really need to be sure you won't be miserable in a certain career.

If you're unsure of what you want to do, there are a couple of different paths you can take, two of which I would recommend. First of all, if you have narrowed your choices down to two or three fields, start with the one that interests you most, and go after it with everything you've got. Only by really going after something are we able to learn what it can offer. The other possible path, if a high-paying position is possible for you, is to try to make and save as much money as possible for a few years. A high-paying job will provide the money you need to either go back to school or to otherwise try various careers without having to be as concerned about money for a while.

73
Treat College Like the Cafeteria of Activities It Is

You will never have better opportunities to try out so many different activities so easily and cheaply as during your college years. During the school year, these opportunities can range from outdoor activities to hosting radio shows to intramural sports. College clubs often require very little, if any, commitment, so you can try hanging out with many of them to see what works for you. Many club- or school-sponsored events are subsidized, so take advantage of them.

Summers can be times for paid or unpaid internships, living in another area cheaply, or travel. You are not likely to have experiences after college when your expenses, including rent, will be so low. In fact, many students will live at home during the summer and not pay rent. Be sure this is the best option for you, as there are often better opportunities and more attractive options for growth by going away from home for one or more summers. Look into what's available, and make the most of this opportunity-filled time of your life!

74
Take Advantage of Great Exchange Rates

Some of the most amazing deals during college are the exchange programs, where trying out a different school in the same country, or even another country, doesn't cost much more than a regular quarter or semester at your current school! The programs are usually structured to include travel and lodging, the latter of which can especially be a challenge to find on your own.

Don't underestimate the value of domestic exchange programs. Domestic programs are largely overlooked in favor of the international programs, as going to another country is such an exciting opportunity and often such a great deal, but domestic programs offer benefits as well. For example, you could try out living in a different part of the country, or you might be able to do an undergraduate exchange program at a university that has a graduate program in which you have interest. The latter choice would be a great way to show your interest in the school and to make sure it would be the best choice for you.

The international programs are often unbelievably good deals, and allow for extra travel during breaks or before or after the program. Also, the classes that are offered are usually easy relative to classes at home, allowing students the time and energy to explore on their own.

75
Appreciate Your Peers

One of the biggest changes after college is that you will no longer be around a group that is so close in age and has such flexible schedules. Keep this in mind and make the most of your social options during your time in school. Making friends may get harder as years go on, and having a good core group of friends from college can make the transition into the working world easier and more enjoyable, especially if some of them move to the same area as you after graduation. College is possibly the last time of your life when you'll be around thousands of other people in your age group every day, and that's not something to be taken for granted! In fact, sometimes I wonder what percentage of graduate school applicants want to go back to school just to get back even a little of that experience.

※

76
Enjoy the Anticipation of Coming Home

If you go away to a four-year college right after high school, there's a really nice benefit when it comes time for holidays. You might not really get this point until you've both experienced and lost it, but coming home from school and seeing all your old friends is a great feeling. Something about the combination of starting an exciting new life and having so much to talk about mixed with a little homesickness can draw old friends closer.

The breaks you'll get at Thanksgiving are often especially sweet, as most people generally only have family obligations on that Thursday night, and a lot of people are available to hang out on Friday and Saturday (and sometimes even Wednesday). If you want to see people you went to high school with, head out on the Friday and Saturday night after Thanksgiving.

There's no time like the college years and maybe a year or two after to see all of your old friends at the local bars and other hangouts. Take advantage of this, because it won't last. People will move away, get married, have children, otherwise scatter, and become more difficult to bring together. Appreciate these years as they happen as well as taking pictures and videos of the good times, and you'll have memories to last a lifetime.

77
Discover the Truth About Teamwork

While it is important to learn to work with others, chances are that the importance of teamwork will be overestimated in college and the importance of independent work will be underestimated. Working effectively with others is definitely important, but it's also very important to be able to get work done independently. Companies often stress the importance of teamwork, but what is usually meant is the ability to get along with others. The most common situation is for teams to come together in a meeting, and then for individuals to go off to complete the work on their own. Be able to communicate that you can work well both on teams and by yourself when you do job interviews, and if you can back this up, your employers will be happy to have hired you.

78
Find Work Opportunities Designed for New Grads

Some truth exists in the oft-repeated lament, "I can't get a job without experience, but I can't get experience without a job." Internships are probably the best remedy for this, but another solution is to look for companies that actively seek out graduating college students for management or other training programs. Management consulting companies are a good example of this.

Companies are interested in graduating students for a combination of factors. For one thing, new graduates are seen as easier to train by some companies, as the students haven't yet developed entrenched ideas about how things should be done. Second, college graduates tend to have a lot of energy and are often willing to pay dues with grunt work, long hours, and relatively low pay. Lastly, and especially key for consulting companies, young graduates tend to not yet have families and are therefore more amenable to travel and relocation.

Your school's career center should have a good sense of the companies looking for students to hire right out of school, as these are likely to be the companies the career center is in contact with for career fairs and internships. Seek out these companies and jobs, and you can set yourself up for a great career path, possibly even putting yourself quickly ahead of others who have more experience.

79
Enjoy the Ride as Time Speeds Up

If there's one thing I can tell you with near-certainty, it's that time seems to accelerate as life goes on. Go after what you want when you're young and have the energy and the flexibility. Trust me when I say that your 20's will go by in a flash. Act deliberately to have the time to travel and have fun while still laying the groundwork for a rewarding career. If you're willing to continue learning over time, life can just get better and better, as you'll learn from your mistakes and build upon your successes. I hope this book has helped you gain a sense of what it takes to succeed in college and beyond.

Good luck, and have fun!

Printed in Great Britain
by Amazon